C

The story of the
BICYCLE

by EDMUND HUNTER

with illustrations by
RONALD JACKSON MSIA

Publishers: Ladybird Books Ltd . Loughborough
© Ladybird Books Ltd 1975
Printed in England

The first bicycles

A drawing by the great inventor Leonardo da Vinci
which was recently found in Italy shows what is
probably the earliest design for a bicycle. The drawing,
dated 1493, clearly shows a two wheeled machine with
saddle, handlebars and pedals. Perhaps the most
significant feature of da Vinci's design is the use of
toothed gear wheels and a chain, a method of propulsion
not actually used until about 1870.

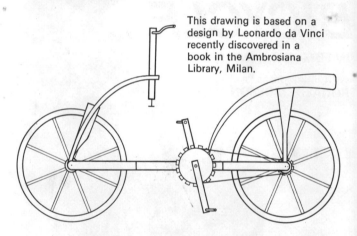

This drawing is based on a
design by Leonardo da Vinci
recently discovered in a
book in the Ambrosiana
Library, Milan.

About 300 years after da Vinci's death, a French
nobleman, named Count de Sivrac, invented a machine
which he showed to the public in Paris about 1790. It
was known as the celerifere and was really an enlarged
version of a children's toy which had been in use for
many years. It consisted of a wooden frame with two

wheels, and was supposed to represent a wooden horse. Some models even had a horse's head carved at the front.

These early machines proved difficult to ride mainly because they were not equipped with a steering mechanism. Forward movement was produced by the rider pushing with his feet against the ground. Iron rimmed wheels, hard wooden seats and rough French roads must have made riding the celerifere an uncomfortable experience.

It was not until 1816 that a steerable machine was developed.

The French Celeripede

Hobby-horse

The velocipede

The celerifere was later renamed the velocipede and was for a time an amusing, if uncomfortable, form of transport in fashionable Parisian circles.

Machines without proper steering were, however, very limited in their use. The velocipede and its like might well have died at an early age had not a German, Baron Karl von Drais, invented front-wheel steering. He also provided his machines with armrests for the rider to lean on and so enable him to push harder with his feet. There was padding for the seat to add a little more comfort.

Two variations of the 'Draisienne'.

The ideas of von Drais were taken up and developed, in Great Britain, by Denis Johnson. His machine was patented under the name 'Pedestrian Curricle'.

These machines were made of wood; they were heavy and awkward to push along. The roads on which they were used were rough and often muddy. In spite of all this, speeds of eight to nine miles per hour were claimed and journeys of up to fifty miles were tackled. This says much for the stamina and determination of those first 'cyclists'.

MODERN PEGASUS or *Dandy Hobbies in full Speed* *Pub Mar 24 1819 by J. ... Cheapside*

Arm power as well as foot power

With the introduction of the steering mechanism, a major problem had been overcome. The inventors now turned their attention to another problem, that of propulsion.

This particular aspect of cycling had provided cartoonists of the day with good subjects for their humorous drawings, and prompted one writer to make the following observation: "The new Irish Jaunting Car, the Dandy's Hobby, the Velocipede or the Perambulator, by which you can ride at your EASE and are obliged to walk in the mud at the same time."

In 1821 an Englishman named Lewis Gompertz devised a means of using arm power to supplement foot power. It worked by means of a toothed rack acting on a pinion fixed to the axle of the front wheel. Therefore by pushing the steering lever to and fro the front wheel turned.

These strange and cumbersome machines of the early nineteenth century at last provided an alternative to walking and horse-drawn transport.

The cartoon reproduced opposite is typical of the treatment that the cyclists of that time received at the hands of the cartoonists and other humourists.

Lewis Gompertz with his Velocipede

The first rear-wheel drive

A Scottish blacksmith named Kirkpatrick Macmillan was the first person to make a pedal-driven bicycle, in about 1840. He fitted a pair of pedals to his hobby-horse and connected them, with an arrangement of cranks and levers, to the rear wheel. His machine weighed 57 lbs (26 kg), had a wheelbase of 48 ins (122 cm), a front wheel diameter of 32 ins (81 cm) and a rear wheel diameter of $42\frac{1}{2}$ ins (108 cm). His design also incorporated a brake operated by a twist-grip on the handlebar.

On this machine Macmillan could reach a speed of 10 mph (16 kph) and sometimes, on short sprints, 14 mph (23 kph). He was also able to outrun the local stagecoach, much to the disgust of both driver and passengers.

Macmillan also had another first. At the end of a forty mile ride on his machine he was involved in an accident with a child. He was fined five shillings by a local magistrate for reckless driving.

The Scotsman's pedal-driven bicycle was not a great success. The system of cranks was too complicated and the friction caused by the clumsy joints wasted too much of the rider's power. It was a beginning and a way had been found to propel a bicycle without the rider having to put his feet on the ground.

The reckless driving
Kirkpatrick Macmilla

Front-wheel drive

The next important stage in the development of the bicycle took place in 1861. A Frenchman, Pierre Michaux of Paris, thought of fitting cranks and pedals directly to the axle of the front wheel. His son Ernest put this idea into practice and it worked so well that it was quickly taken up in other countries. In America, a manufacturing company was set up in Connecticut to make the new models.

Although the idea was a great success it did suffer from having too low a 'gear ratio'. This meant that one turn of the pedals would advance the machine a distance equal to the circumference of the front wheel, only about 10 ft (3 m). (A modern bicycle, by using gears, will cover 16 ft (5 m) or more.) This meant that to achieve even moderate speeds the rider would have to pedal quite quickly, and therefore would rapidly become exhausted.

It was this problem that led inventors and engineers to consider the whole question of 'gear ratio' and the distance travelled for each turn of the pedals.

In spite of this drawback, the popularity of the bicycle grew in France, but it was not until many years later that bicycles became common in England.

Reynolds & May
'Phantom' bicycle
1869

Treadle-driven tricycle 1850

Machines of many kinds

As cycling increased in popularity more and more
people took to the open air. The exercise, though hard,
was healthy. Soon a wide variety of machines made
their appearance. There were two, three and four
wheelers, as well as one, two and three seaters.

Methods of propulsion consisted mainly of arm power
and leg power though one extraordinary design was
actually propelled by dog power. The two large driving
wheels were made in the form of cages and each
contained a dog which worked 'treadmill fashion' to
move the vehicle forward. The more unusual machines

were not taken seriously by the public, who often regarded them as the product of some of the more unorthodox inventors. Such machines were often very impractical and soon disappeared from the roads.

Meanwhile, the two-wheeled versions went from strength to strength. Schools were formed in the main centres of population throughout Europe and America, where the art of cycling could be taught. Many people performed stunts such as riding with 'no hands' and standing on the saddle. Such activities are, of course, not allowed on our roads today with their fast-moving traffic and other dangers, but in those early days were regarded as novel and entertaining.

r-wheeled velocipede

Country tricycle 1876

Cycle racing begins

In the twenty years between 1850 and 1870 standards of riding improved and cycle racing became a popular and fashionable sport. The first officially recorded race was held at St. Cloud Park in Paris on May 31st, 1868. The event, run over a distance of 1200 metres (1312 yds) was won by an Englishman named James Moore, who beat Drouet and Policini. James Moore also won the first real road race, in 1869, from Paris to Rouen. This race attracted about two hundred entries and was started by the Miss America of that time. Cycling enthusiasts will know that the Paris to Rouen race is still run to this day as an annual event for amateur riders.

Moore was the most successful rider of his time, winning as many as five World Championships, a considerable achievement on a machine with direct pedal drive to the front wheel and no gears. He also won the English Mile Championship at the Molyneux ground in the Midlands, which is now the home of Wolverhampton Wanderers Football Club.

Road racing of all kinds was organised by the ever growing number of cycling clubs, and closed tracks were built all over the world. The sport generally attracted quite large crowds of excited spectators.

James Moore winning
at St. Cloud Park

The high bicycle

In the early 1870s wood construction had given way to iron and steel, and a great many other developments took place.

The need for higher speeds led to the introduction of the large front driving wheel. These machines were called 'High' or 'Ordinary' bicycles, commonly known today as 'Penny Farthings'. Probably the first of these was the 'Ariel', made by James Starley of Coventry in 1870, which sold for £12.

To demonstrate the possibilities of these machines a party of four people set out from London to cycle to John o'Groats in 1873. They covered the 861 miles (1386 km) in 15 days.

The racing high bicycles of the time had a front wheel diameter of about 50 ins (127 cm), although some were as large as 60 ins (152 cm). This continuing quest for speed led designers to make even larger wheels. One cycling magazine of the time proudly announced the '7 feet Ariel', a front wheel diameter of 84 ins (213 cm). To propel one of these giants would have been a physical impossibility without the use of special pedal extensions.

Most of the high bicycles were fitted with solid rubber tyres and also had brakes and springs. Although they were heavy, weighing between 40 lbs (18 kg) and 50 lbs (23 kg), they were still a big improvement on the wooden velocipedes of a few years earlier.

Bicycle rac
in the 187

19

If the assistance of a friendly arm or stand of suitable height was not available, mounting was a tricky operation.

Mounting

There were two methods of mounting. The first was to run by the left side of the machine, put the left foot on the step and swing the right leg up over the seat. The second and more difficult method was to stand with the left foot on the step and start hopping until the rider had enough speed to raise himself onto the step and swing his right leg across the seat.

Dismounting

To-dismount, the rider had to swing his left leg backwards onto the step, and then raise his right leg up over.the seat and onto the ground.

Riding the high bicycle

Mounting the high bicycle was done with the aid of a step fixed just above the small rear wheel. It was not an easy operation. Learners were advised to ask a friend to hold the machine steady while they got on, or to mount near a wall so that the bicycle could be supported.

Riding too could be quite dangerous. The roads were often rough and an unexpected bump might cause the rider to fall from his high seat. Going down hill, particularly at speed, was another problem. A few machines were fitted with footrests so that the cyclist could allow the machine to free-wheel. This was not advised unless the rider could see to the bottom of the hill in case he had to get off the machine in a hurry.

Another piece of advice was that cyclists should "have their drawers lined smoothly and carefully with chamois leather, or buckskin, before proceeding on a long journey." The discomforts of cycling were not confined to falling off.

Bicycles and tricycles from Coventry

It was the fact that the high bicycle was difficult to mount and ride that prompted the development of the tricycle during the 1870s. Ladies of the day were invited to use these three wheelers, which were thought to be more suitable than their two wheeled counterparts. Even Queen Victoria ordered two 'Royal Salvo' tricycles, thereby helping to make the new craze of cycling more respectable.

In Britain, at this time, Coventry had become the main centre of bicycle manufacture, the Coventry Machinists Company making the greatest number of models.

James Starley being presented to Queen Victoria at Osbourne in 1881 in the presence of Prince Leopold, Princess Beatrice and Sir Henry Ponsonby, the Queen's Private Secretary. Pictured in the foreground is one of the 'Royal Salvo' tricycles purchased by the Queen.

Factories were expanding to deal with the ever increasing demand for bicycles, and this was the beginning of the British cycle industry, which started in Coventry and in more recent times moved to Nottingham.

Perhaps the most famous name in the Coventry cycle trade, at that time, was that of James Starley, designer of the 'Royal Salvo' tricycle and 'Ariel' high bicycle. In fact, it was J. K. Starley, a nephew of James, whom we have to thank for the bicycle as we know it today.

J. K. Starley on the
Rover Safety Cycle

The safety bicycle

In 1878 J. K. Starley formed a partnership with a man
named William Sutton, to develop and produce tricycles.
However in 1885 Starley designed, independently, his
'Rover Safety Bicycle'. This machine is widely regarded
as being the final step in the development of the bicycle
form. It consisted of a simple diamond-shaped frame
and two wheels of equal diameter with the rear one
driven by a chain. The basic design of modern bicycles
differs very little from that of Starley's machine.

An advertisement of the time described the Rover as
"Safer than any tricycle, faster and easier than any

bicycle ever made. Fitted with handles to turn for convenience in storing and shipping. Far and away the best hill-climber in the market."

It is perhaps interesting to note that in Germany at this time a man named Gottlieb Daimler, of later car fame, had equipped a bicycle with an internal combustion engine, thus producing the forerunner of the modern motorcycle.

A cartoon of 1885 by George Moore, entitled Battle of the Safeties, shows the Rover Safety Cycle in competition with the front driven Kangaroo Safety Cycle.

Rover Safety Cycle
Kangaroo front driven Safety Cycle

'Ivel' Racing Safety
Bicycle 1886

H. J. Lawson's Safety
'Bicyclette' 1879

Humber Safety
Bicycle 1884

Other chain-driven bicycles

Starley's designs were very much in demand and created
a cycling boom in Britain. He even changed the name
of his company to the Rover Company Ltd.

Although the Rover design popularised chain-driven
bicycles, there were several others before it, some of
which are shown above.

The McCammon Safety Bicycle of 1884 was particularly
suitable for ladies, due to its drop frame design. This
was also a feature of the Ivel, built in 1886 by Don
Albone.

J. McCammon Safety
Bicycle 1884

B.S.A. Safety
Bicycle 1884

Lindley & Biggs
'Whippet'
Safety Bicycle 1888

The spring framed Whippet was introduced in 1888 by Lindley and Biggs. It was thought that by incorporating flexible joints and springs into the frame, the rider would be insulated from the bumps of the road. The development of the pneumatic tyre a few years later put a premature end to this ingenious device.

The B.S.A. Safety Bicycle was made in the Midlands by the Birmingham Small Arms Company, a firm of rifle makers seeking work to keep their staff fully employed. This company went on to become one of the major bicycle and motor-cycle manufacturers in Britain.

The bicycle in America

If the main advancement of the early bicycle took place in Britain and Europe, America was certainly not far behind. A man named Albert A. Pope became as important in that country as Starley was in England.

Pope, a retired army officer, was a carriage builder. He began by importing British high bicycles before starting his own company in 1878. At one time his was the largest bicycle factory in the world and it was there that the idea of mass production was first introduced. Henry Ford later adopted the same ideas in the manufacture of his motor cars. Of course, nearly all cars and a great many other things are made by the mass production system today.

On one occasion Pope hired Will Pitman, Maryland 'Boneshaker' Champion, to demonstrate one of his bicycles. During the demonstration a horse was frightened by the machine, and the cyclist was promptly arrested. Pope gained a lot of publicity from this event, and went on to develop the American cycle industry and provide help for the American cyclist, arranging races and working to get the roads improved. He was also a founder member of the League of American Wheelmen, an organisation still in existence today.

Round the world on a bicycle

On April 22nd, 1884 Thomas Stevens left San Francisco, on a high bicycle with solid tyres, to cycle round the world. He completed his journey on January 4th, 1887.

1 10th May 1884. Meets mountain lion in United States.

2 13th-15th May 1885. In Paris, France.

5 24th June 1885. In Bulgaria, meeting the Bulgarian Express.

6 22nd July 1885. In Istanbul, Turkey.

9 17th-24th April 1886. Arrested in Afghanistan, and returned to Persia.

10 2nd August 1886. In Amritsar, India.

3 24th May 1885. In Germany.

4 1st-3rd June 1885. Through Austria and Hungary.

7 16th-17th August 1885. Approaching Ankara, Turkey.

8 30th September 1885 - 10th March 1886. In Teheran, Persia.

11 13th October 1886. Near Canton, in China.

12 28th November 1886. On Shimonoseki Ferry in Japan.

31

Troubled times for cyclists

Not all sections of the public were as keen on bicycles as were the cyclists themselves. There was a great deal of antagonism between those who rode bicycles and those who drove horse carriages. It was quite common for a carriage driver to lash out with his whip at any cyclist who dared to overtake him.

Other troubles arose when innkeepers refused to serve some cyclists who arrived tired and dirty after pedalling along the dusty or muddy roads. Children in particular enjoyed upsetting riders by poking sticks through the spokes of their wheels.

In France it was not unknown for glass and tin tacks to be spread across the road causing havoc to the rather fragile pneumatic tyres of the time, and for farmers to completely block the roads with their carts.

In 1878 the Bicycle Touring Club was formed by an Englishman named Stanley Cotterell. Five years later this became the Cyclists Touring Club. This organisation still looks after the interests of cyclists in Britain and arranges cycling events as it did nearly 100 years ago. The initials C.T.C. are world famous.

The pneumatic tyre

One of the most important developments in the evolution of the bicycle, and in road transport in general, took place in 1888. This was the addition of the pneumatic (or air-filled) tyre to the wheel by John Boyd Dunlop, a Scottish veterinary surgeon living in Ireland.

Dunlop sought a way to make his son's cycling faster and more comfortable. With this in mind he conducted a simple experiment. He cut out two discs of solid wood, one being slightly smaller than the other. To the smaller one he fitted an inflated air tube protected by a strip

of canvas nailed to the sides of the wheel. By rolling both the discs along the ground he observed that the pneumatic tyred disc travelled further than the plain wooden one.

One day when his son's pneumatic tyred tricycle was parked outside a hotel, a crowd of 400 or 500 people crowded round trying to obtain a sight of it.

Soon after this Dunlop formed a company to make his pneumatic tyres.

The growing popularity of the bicycle

Dunlop's development of the pneumatic tyre took some of the hard work and discomfort out of cycling and so increased the appeal of the bicycle as an everyday means of transport. Postmen, policemen, soldiers, doctors, nurses and delivery boys all found the bicycle to be a quick and convenient way of getting about. In the past everyone either had to walk, travel on horseback or in some horse-drawn vehicle. A bicycle was cheaper than a horse and trap, and required much less looking after than a horse.

Ladies as well as gentlemen found cycling to their liking even though their long, wide skirts were always in

danger of getting caught up in the chain and spokes.
The skirts were also rather heavy and made pedalling
difficult. This problem was overcome by the introduction
of the 'bloomer', an adaptation of a garment worn in
the Far East for centuries. This idea was popularised by
a woman named Elizabeth Miller, but the new garment
was named after Amelia Bloomer whose name seemed
more appropriate to the costume. It caused a sensation
when introduced in about 1851, and soon became the
fashion amongst the ladies of the day.

Distance travelled by one turn of the pe[dals]

Velocipede of 1861 - With the pedals attached directly to the front wheel, the distance travelled equalled the circumference of the wheel.

High Bicycle of 1871 - The obvious way to increase this distance was to increase the size of the wheel.

Safety Bicycle 1888 - Because they used gears these machines no longer needed the large driving wheel.

New inventions

The cycle industry was now booming and thousands of companies were engaged in it. Inventors all over the world worked to make improvements in the design and mechanical details of the machines. Some of these developments are still in use today but they are now much more efficient than their predecessors.

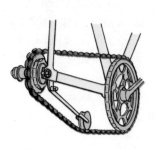

Free-wheel
The free-wheel is an old invention, its first known application to a bicycle was b[y] Lewis Gompertz in 1821. Its first use as a standard item on a safety bicycle was in 1895.

Lindley and Biggs two spee[d] gear
This two speed gear was introduced in about 1900. It worked by using a specially shaped chain running over wid[e] chain wheels, that allowed it t[o] move from one gear to the other. The design also incorporated a pulley to take u[p] the slack when the chain was on the smaller gear.

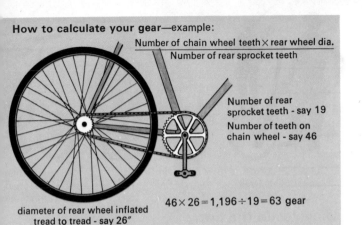

How to calculate your gear—example:

$$\frac{\text{Number of chain wheel teeth} \times \text{rear wheel dia.}}{\text{Number of rear sprocket teeth}}$$

Number of rear sprocket teeth - say 19

Number of teeth on chain wheel - say 46

diameter of rear wheel inflated tread to tread - say 26"

$46 \times 26 = 1,196 \div 19 = 63$ gear

Derailleur gears

This system of gear changing used sprockets of various sizes and the chain could be moved from one sprocket to another to give a higher or lower gear.

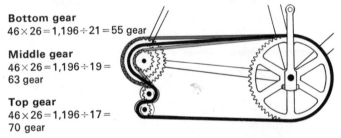

Bottom gear
$46 \times 26 = 1,196 \div 21 = 55$ gear

Middle gear
$46 \times 26 = 1,196 \div 19 = 63$ gear

Top gear
$46 \times 26 = 1,196 \div 17 = 70$ gear

In California in 1944, whilst trying to break the World Mile record, Alfred Letourner used a gear of 252. He covered the mile in a time of 33.05 seconds, a speed of 108.92 mph, riding behind a wind-shield attached to a racing car.

39

Dursley Pederson
bicycle British 1899

Captain Gerard
bicycle French 1896

Military folding
bicycle German.
Late 19th century

Bicycles in the army

Transport is very important for an army and the bicycle
has played its part in peace and war.

The Italian army had some bicycles as far back as 1870,
and before 1900 the French were using folding bicycles
which soldiers could carry on their backs when
conditions were not suitable for riding. British
cycle-firms developed machine-gun carrying tricycles
and quadricycles.

Of course, the bicycle was never able to take the place
of the horse in wartime as it often did in civilian life.
There were certain types of country where it could not
be ridden, such as long grass and mud.

Folding bicycles in use by
French troops during the
2nd World War

On the other hand it was light enough to be carried or dragged along until a better surface was reached.

As recently as the second World War, folding bicycles were used by some paratroops to give them greater speed of movement when they landed on the ground. The silent running of the bicycle was also very convenient when making surprise attacks.

Folding bicycles in use by assault troops during the 2nd World War

Silent wartime transport

Both folding and non-folding bicycles were successfully used by British troops in the second World War. The advantage of this fast silent form of transport was also exploited by underground forces in many occupied countries.

B.S.A. folding bicycle 1940

Steam-driven bicycle Michaux & Perreaux 1869

This steam-driven bicycle was built in 1869 by Pierre Michaux, using a Perreaux steam engine.

The light weight of the bicycle offered possibilities that were later developed with the internal-combustion engine.

Daimler motor bicycle 1885

This strange-looking vehicle was the forerunner of the modern motorcycle. It was designed and built by Gottlieb Daimler in 1885.

It was powered by a single-cylinder internal-combustion engine. The two small wheels lifted up once the bicycle was on the move.

Benz motor tricycle 1885

Carl Benz included many advanced features in this forerunner of the modern motor car, including electric ignition, effective throttle control, mechanical valves and a horizontal flywheel. It also had a comfortable upholstered seat.

The de-luxe bicycle 1901

The turn of the century saw two main developments in the bicycle industry. One was the attachment of motorised power to adapted bicycles, to create the examples you see on this page.

The other was the perfection of the conventional bicycle. The 'Golden' Sunbeam bicycle resulted from greatly improved manufacturing techniques and the patronage of the wealthier classes. It was so good, it remained almost unaltered from 1902 to 1936.

The Sunbeam Mabley 1901 This four-wheeled vehicle with two forward gears and 'tiller' steering, was a popular development from the bicycle.

The famous 'Golden' Sunbeam bicycle, with two speed gear, stirrup-type brakes and beaded-edge pneumatic tyres.

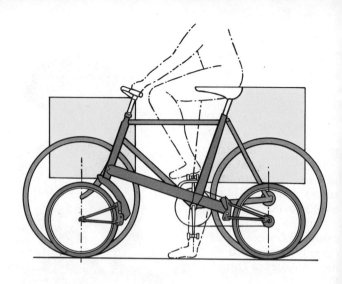

The Moulton bicycle

Perhaps the most significant development in recent years
has been the introduction of the small-wheeled Moulton
bicycle.

The first prototype was made in 1959, being followed by
many others until August 1962 when the design was
finalised.

Above is the original drawing, showing the smaller
wheels, the 40:60 weight distribution, the early design
for the front and rear suspension and the increased
carrying space caused by the small wheels.

The Moulton went into production in 1962, and in 1970
underwent a globe-trotting test, being ridden from
England to Singapore in 5 months by Colin Martin.

His special machine weighed 68 lbs (31 kg) and used only five tyres during the journey.

Other manufacturers quickly saw the potential of the Moulton and soon introduced similar machines, the principal one being the Raleigh RSW16.

The Moulton has also helped, along with the fuel crisis, to check the decline in bicycle sales, and cycling is now enjoying a world-wide upsurge in popularity, making us healthier, wealthier and more free in these days of overcrowded roads.

The Tour de France. 1974

The most famous bicycle race in the world is the Tour de France. In 1974 the event started from Brest in northern France and, for the first time, visited England where a race of 102 miles (163 km) was held at Plymouth. The event finished in Paris, having covered a total distance of 4,412 miles (7100 km).

This page shows the cyclists climbing the Galibier Pass in the French Alps which rises to a height of 8,000 ft (2438 m).

Results :
1. **Eddy Merckx**
   Team Molteni
2. **Raymond Poulidor**
   Team Gan Mercier
3. **Vincente Lopez-Carril**
   Team Kas

England

France

Spain

Key:
1. E. Merckx
2. R. Poulidor
3. V. Lopez-Carril
4. P. Sercu
5. B. Hoban
6. T.V. Cameraman
7. Team Car
8. Judges Car

47

Correct frame size
There are a great many frame shapes and sizes available today, and it is important to choose one that is right for the individual rider. A child should be able to touch the ground with the balls of his feet when seated on the machine.

Saddle height
The saddle should be adjusted so that the rider can touch the ground with both feet, whilst seated, and also be able to put one heel on a pedal in the down position.

Maintenance

It is very important to check your bicycle regularly for roadworthiness, as any mechanical fault could make it dangerous to ride. All the moving parts should be oiled often, so that they work smoothly and quietly. Also check all the nuts and screws for tightness. The brakes should be kept in peak condition, as your life may depend on your being able to stop in an emergency.

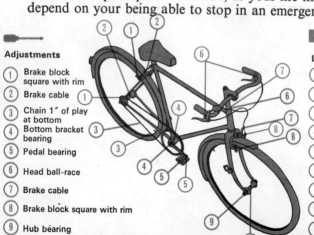

Adjustments

1. Brake block square with rim
2. Brake cable
3. Chain 1″ of play at bottom
4. Bottom bracket bearing
5. Pedal bearing
6. Head ball-race
7. Brake cable
8. Brake block square with rim
9. Hub bearing

Lubricate

1. Freewheel
2. Hub bearing
3. Chain
4. Bottom bracket bearing
5. Pedal bearing
6. Brake lever
7. Head bearing
8. Brake caliper
9. Hub bearing

djustments of heights

aving adjusted the saddle height,
e handle-bar height should be
e-adjusted so that the rider, when
eated, should be leaning slightly
orward. Further adjustments may
e made to enable the rider to feel
vell balanced and comfortable.

Pedalling or ankling

No matter how good your
bicycle is, you will not achieve
the best results until you can
pedal correctly.

1. As you press
downwards and forwards
with one foot, rest the
other as it is lifted.

2. Your feet should
be kept in the correct
position by ankling,
i.e. the up and down
movement of your toes
from the ankle. This is
one of the secrets of
easy cycling.

3. The foot that has been
pressing downwards is
about to be lifted upwards
during its rest period.
To ride well you need to
pedal properly.

Individual positions

It is important to have the seat
and handle-bars correctly
adjusted to obtain the safest and
most efficient riding position.

1. The handle-bars are too low
in relation to the saddle,
putting too much weight on
the wrists and producing a
head down position.

2. The handle-bars are too high
in relation to the saddle,
putting all your weight on
the saddle and none on the
handle-bars.

3. The correct position, with the
rider leaning slightly forward
and the weight shared
between handle-bars and
saddle.

**The National
Cycling
Proficiency
Scheme**

Under this scheme more than 3 million
cyclists have been trained since 1959.
Training sessions are usually provided
by local authorities and supervised by
road safety officers. After training
children must take an official test to
obtain the National Cycling
Proficiency Certificate and Badge.

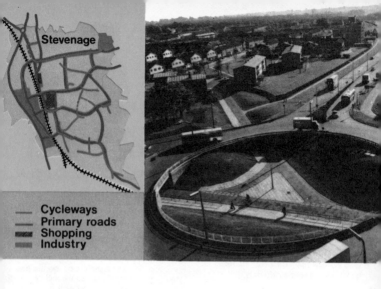

_____ Cycleways
_____ Primary roads
▨▨▨ Shopping
▬▬▬ Industry

Cycling in towns and cities

With the ever increasing popularity of the bicycle it
would seem logical to improve and increase the facilities
afforded to the cyclist. The dangers of mixing with heavy
traffic on main roads can be overcome by the use of
'cycle only' roads, called cycleways.

Stevenage, a new town in Hertfordshire, is a good example
of what can be done with careful planning. A network
of cycleways from residential areas to schools, shops,

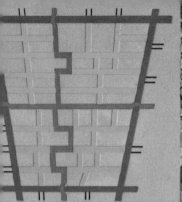

Cycle priority route
Motorways
Access route for cycles
and cars

offices and factories is
provided and it is
estimated that Stevenage
has saved £60,000 per
annum in hospital
expenses as a result of
their scheme: a large
saving both financially
and in terms of human
suffering.

The illustrations on this
page are based on a plan
for a 'Cycle Priority Route'
in Nottingham, the idea
being that certain roads
would be open mainly to
bicycles; other vehicles
would have only limited
access.

HOW TO MEND A PUNCTURE

1 See if you can find what has caused the puncture.

2 Insert tyre lever between wh rim and tyre, lift edge of tyre over rim.

3 Insert another tyre lever 6 ins (15 cm) from first one and lever tyre off.

4 Slide second lever round wh rim, removing one tyre edge completely.

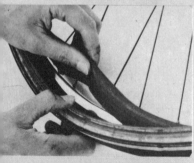

5 Carefully remove inner-tube from inside tyre.

6 Unscrew valve lock-nut, pus valve through wheel rim and remove inner-tube. Check ins of tyre for cause of puncture.